Wolf in
CHEF'S
Clothing

Wolf

in CHEF'S Clothing

by Robert H. Loeb, Jr.
illustrated by Jim Newhall

THE picture COOK AND DRINK BOOK FOR MEN

Wilcox & Follett Company   CHICAGO NEW YORK

table of contents

dedication

To my father, and my father's father, and my father's father's father, right back to Adam, all of whom spent their lives as the passive victims of feminine culinary caprice—from that first apple to apfelstrudel.

And to the little woman, too, and the middle-sized woman, and the big woman—in fact, all women; the connubial-bliss type and the convivial-miss type, all of whom have been tangled for centuries in the maze of cookbook hieroglyphics, cuneiform and Sanscrit.

measuring symbols

That's all—nothing more to it. *No teaspoons at all*, no fractional "ozzes," converting litres to quarts—no special measuring instruments of any kind. If you're worried about exactly how much a tablespoon is, forget it. Just use an ordinary one, and fill it up above level. The same applies for a cup. And for half of either, just be approximate. The art of cooking, like the art of love-making, depends more on the proper use of ingredients than on their exact quantitative measurements. So relax, wolf, when you mix, and bark joyously when you stir. Never be tense and growl; remember in order to make that dish you're supposed to be placid like the sheep—a veritable lamb. Get what I mean, old chop?

cooking with pictures

THERE probably have been as many cookbooks written as there are recipes. Tomes printed in fine type for wives, matrons, chefs, gourmets —about what Martha Washington served, Mom's favorite dishes, the "Selected Recipes of the Confederated Clubs of All-Women Members of Apidula, North Carolina," etc., etc.

No one really ever considered the male animal who didn't want to know how to prepare carp according to a rare Tibetan, or pore through a hundred lines of instructions so that he could turn out the dessert that Madame de Pompadour served Louis XV on September 18, 1748. In fact, no one ever considered that man, a man (except, of course, Louis), is just as anxious, and under just as much obligation, to be a good host as woman is to be a hostess. He's equally as desirous of knowing how to prepare simple, pleasing dishes —or drinks—for friend or "femme."

9

The purpose of this book is to enfranchise the male, to unshackle him from the role of refrigerator vulture, icebox scavenger, from being a parasitic gourmet forced to feed on the leftovers of female cookery. Instead, he can become a gustatory eagle, king of the kitchen, and baron of the bar.

And where does he go from there? He can shine as a host by being able to serve custom-made snacks and drinks, not factory-made ones. He'll no longer be a slave to the maître d'hôtel—he'll be his own. And think of the money he'll save. And if he's a married man, consider the scope this new art can give him. For state occasions, anniversaries, birthdays, Mother's Days, guilt and appeasement days, he won't just be limited to flowers and mink. He'll be able to serve a brunch, a supper, or a breakfast fit for a queen—and let her do the dishes for a change. It's a saving all around. In fact, he'll be able to make a simple dish for every occasion—midday, midnight, maid's night off, and for some special persuasion.

And how is this magical transformation of the male animal accomplished? The instructions in the average cookbook are as terrifying as those on an income-tax form. While you're wrestling with some fragile eggs in one hand, you're to refer back to Paragraph C, Section 39 (you have to turn back three pages with the other hand to do that, too) and, at the same time, you are to measure out three milligrams of baking powder with some astral third hand, constantly stirring the sauce that's supposed to be simmering—but seems to be singeing—with yet a fourth hand. That's all right for an octopus, but who wants to be an octopus? A squid. But that sort of multimanual activity is not for man.

Instead, all impractical recipes have been sifted out; only those that are of immediate use—simple, tasty, and pleasingly garnished—have been included. The recipes are presented with pictures—wringing out all verbiage —and I mean *all*. The modern, unshackled man can throw out all measurements such as grams, "ozzes" (ounces), milligrams, quarts, litres, and apothecary scales. While you're cooking or mixing even a complicated dish or drink, you don't have to read through line after line of fine type to find out what your next step is. It's all right there in picture form, step by step. You can see at a glance from conception to perfection what the dish is going to be.

And what's more, all recipes are catalogued for the occasion. You don't have to pore through page after page of occult reading matter to figure out what to serve. If you want to make breakfast, turn to the breakfast section. For lunch, supper, midnight snacks, ditto. And drinks—it's a tickler deciding when to serve what. WOLF IN CHEF'S CLOTHING takes over the whole problem by putting drinks in their proper place: drinks for before meals, after meals, in-between meals, and with meals. See what I mean? You don't have to think. All you have to do is make like the pictures.

In fact, all that has been done is to codify the laws of cookery and drinkery in a manner long ago employed by the male animal—then called cave man. He was immortalized because he painted pictures on the walls of his habitat. Here is a return to that technique. Food and drink have been put into cave-man form—with pictures—and thus will open up a vast new realm of social opportunity for bewildered, modern man.

And woman, too.

PART II

breakfast for two

If you want to rise and shine —
     Make her breakfast.
If your conscience is bad —
     Make her breakfast.
If *her* conscience is bad —
     Make her breakfast.
If you want to breakfast her —
     Read on

A male in pajamas is a mussed, woolly, and amorphous thing. Even the best man looks no Don Juan at dawn — just wan. But there's a cure.

coffee – home-brew

drip – looks like this →

ingredients:

procedure:

1. boil

2. put in

3. pour

4. ready when dripped through

percolate – looks like this

ingredients:

procedure:

1. pour

2. put in

3. combine and cover

4. perc

5 min.

14

or **vaculate** — looks like this

ingredients:

procedure:

1. pour

2. put in

3. assemble tightly

4. heat— when H₂O rises to top, turn off flame— when liquid returns to bottom —drink it— it's coffee!

grapefruit

ingredients:

procedure:

1. slice in two

2. cut around segments and trim

3. chill and garnish

strawberries

ingredients: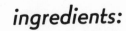

procedure:

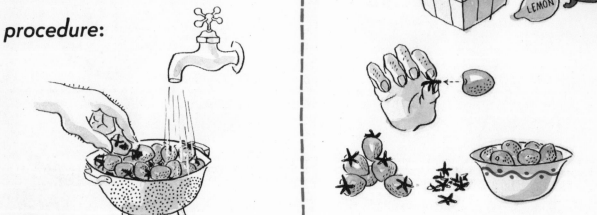

1. wash and pick out bad ones

2. hull

3. sprinkle

4. add and mix

citrous fantasies
or how to juggle an orange

orange Hawaiian

ingredients:

procedure:

1. cut—de—pulp—save shells

2. add to pulp

3. cook till looks like thin marmalade

4. heat's off— mix in

5. fill shells and sprinkle

6. bake—then let cool (not in refrigerator)

CEREALS

oatmeal

ingredients:

procedure:

1. put in and boil

2. add and stir

5 min.

3. transfer to double boiler—

add—cover—cook

1½ HRS.

4. garnish and serve

18

cold and crunchy

the cereal:

or PUFFED WHEAT

Cream

CORN FLAKES

Bran Flakes

or

etc.

the garnish:

sliced or fresh berries or Canned Peaches

Prunes   Apricots

or

etc.

farina

ingredients:

farina   Cream   S   Strawberry Jam

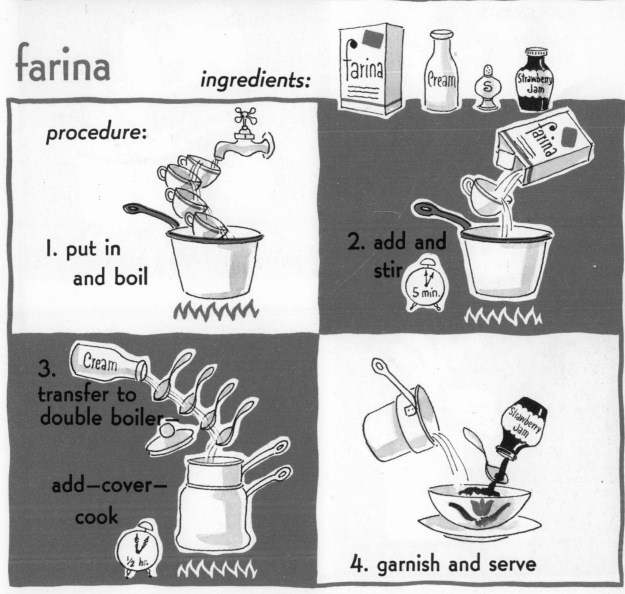

procedure:

1. put in and boil

2. add and stir
5 min.

3. transfer to double boiler

Cream

add—cover— cook
1/2 hr.

Strawberry Jam

4. garnish and serve

scrambled

ingredients:

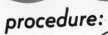

procedure:

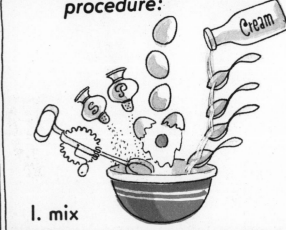

1. mix

2. melt and brown

3. pour and cook—low flame

4. stir until cooked through— serve

Easter scrambled

ingredients:

procedure:

1. mix

2. add and mix

3. melt and brown

4. pour and stir until done

21

shirred eggs

ingredients:

small baking dishes of flameproof glass or earthenware

BUTTER

lemon

PARSLEY

procedure:

1. place in each

250°

2. place and leave until butter is melted

3. remove—slide in without breaking yolks

4. add to each

400°

5. bake until done

PARSLEY

6. remove and garnish—serve

fried eggs

ingredients:

BUTTER

procedure:

1. melt until brown

2. add without breaking yolks!—slow fire

3. off fire when whites are firm—serve (repeat these steps for second batch)

eggs demi-benedict

ingredients:

procedure:

1. cut out with large tumbler and toast

2. cut and fry

3. place and set aside

4. bring to boil

24

5. while waiting for H_2O to boil, mix

6. add yolk only and mix

7. stir—heat very slowly until warm—your sauce is done

8. now to poach—

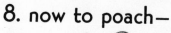

add to boiling water without breaking yolks—low flame

9. when whites solid, transfer gently

10. pour over each—and *voila!*

international
omelet set

French

ingredients:

procedure:

1. mix and beat together

2. melt

3. pour—flame low

4. when solid, flip over—cook one minute—sprinkle

5. remove—roll up—serve *comme* ça

Spanish

ingredients:

procedure:

1. heat

2. chop–
   add–
   cook

5 MIN.

3. add–
   cook
   until it
   thickens

4. make French omelet as on
   preceding page—hurry!

french

5. pour
   one-half
   and roll

french

6. pour
   on
   balance—

serve *con mucho gusto*

American

ingredients:

procedure:

1. separate whites and yolks

2. beat until stiff

3. add—beat

4. blend together—don't beat

5. melt

6. pour—flame low

7. when firm—remove—
place under broiler

8. when top is pale tan,
remove—sprinkle

9. put—roll—serve

pancakes

ingredients:

procedure:

1. mix

2. melt

3. add and mix in

4. in another bowl, mix

5. mix together and add

6. heat and rub on

7. when griddle very hot,
   pour on

8. when full of bubbles,
   flip over

9. remove and serve thus

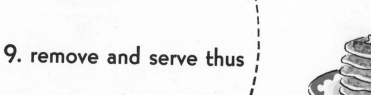

le **toast** de Paris

ingredients:

procedure:

1. mix

2. add and beat in

3. trim and toast *slightly*

4. soak till soggy

5. heat until smoking

6. fry until golden brown

7. drain on paper

8. serve so

32

don't try this unless you have a:

waffles

ingredients:

procedure:

1. separate and beat each

2. mix

3. melt

4. combine by beating

5. mix in gently—don't beat

6. pour on heated iron; remove when crisp tan— serve

33

her majesty's
breakfast service

how to make a queen
eat out of your hand
next time, and
save dishes

proper table setting

proper tray setting

PART III

Here are four $10 specials graded for type:

menu #1

If she's the athletic type—long, lean, and limbsome, who prefers a game of tennis to a shot of 3-star Henness(ey):

tomato juice à l'ocean—mignon et béarnaise—baked potatoes—salad Roquefort

menu #2

If she's the indoor type—soft, round, and fluffy, who thinks Alexander the Great the best cocktail ever made:

broiled grapefruit—lamb chops—potatoes fried à la France—salade Walt Whitman

menu #3

If she's the intellectual type—more an I.Q. than a Q.T.—if she prefers Gounod's *Faust* to getting soused:

orange Hawaiian—spaghetti da Vinci—les choux froids

menu #4

If she's the 3-B type—brains, bonds, and beauty—don't believe it—but it's fun pretending:

strawberry loving cup—poulet maison dixon—potatoes à l'onion—salad subversive

tomato juice à l'océan

ingredients:

procedure:

1. mix

2. add and mix

3. pour and garnish

strawberry loving cup

ingredients:

procedure: 1. make with the orange juice
and strawberries (page 16)

2. combine and stir

3. chill well

4. put in

5. add

broiled grapefruit

ingredients:

procedure:

1. prepare grapefruit

(page 16)

2. sprinkle

3. put under broiler

4. remove—garnish—serve

sea food Dorothea   serves four

ingredients:

procedure:

1. defrost— separate pieces— sprinkle

2. mix in separate bowl

3. add

4. and

5. arrange each portion so

6. pour over each—serve

wolf-fare — the carnivore's baedecker

steak — noble (sir-loin) or t-beian (t-bone)

ingredients:

procedure:

1. sprinkle and spread on each side

2. chop fine

3. fry golden brown—

and meanwhile—

6 MIN.

each side for rare

4. give gas full throttle—place as close to broiler flame as possible—leave door open two inches

5. remove like so

6. mix together— heat one minute

7. pour over—serve

mignon et béarnaise a carnivore's opera

mignon's ingredients:

2 of ←these

1 LB.

TOOTH-PICKS

BUTTER

S P

béarnaise's ingredients:

Taragon Vinegar

Canned Consommé

PAPRIKA

PARSLEY

procedure:

Taragon Vinegar

1. heat—then let cool

2. then separate—discard whites—add yolks—stir

3. now heat in double boiler— stir constantly until smooth

Canned Consommé

4. add and stir

5. add—and keep stir-ring! when smooth, the sauce is done

bacon

tooth-pick

6. now the fillet—wrap around and secure like this—add

7. melt and heat well

8. add

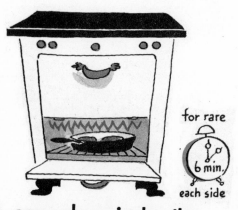

for rare

6 min.

each side

9. now place in broiler

10. remove—pour over—serve

43

lamb chops the amazing meat that goes in like a lamb and comes out like a chop

ingredients:

procedure:

1. thinly smear and add to each side

2. broil each side, full throttle — 1 min.

3. reduce throttle medium, each side — 6 min.

4. meanwhile—melt; add—stir

5. chops done—

remove and pour

6. garnish—serve

poulet  maison dixon

 ingredients:

procedure:

1. cut into joints

2. mix and beat

3. dip each part

4. then roll in

5. heat till smoking

6. fry deep brown

7. remove—drain on paper—serve

spaghetti da Vinci

ingredients:

 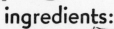    

procedure:

1. heat

2. chop—fry till tan

3. add—mix in

4. add—cook till meat is done

5. remove and transfer

6. add—stir in

7. add—stir in

8. cover—cook slowly

20 minutes before serving

9. put in boiling water

10. remove when soft and drain

11. transfer

12. remove sauce—mix in

13. pour over—sprinkle

14. serve along with

shrimp cobra

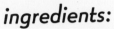

ingredients:

procedure:

1. add to six cups boiling water—cook

2. meanwhile—melt

3. chop—fry till tender

4. add

5. pour juice only—add

6. pour into

cook slowly till slightly thickened

7. add

8. add

9. add—cook slowly

10. now—grease mold well

11. transfer rice—pack in well

12. bake

13. unmold—pour in center

14. serve with

hamburgers *sans* ham

ingredients:

Chopped Round Steak 1½ LBS.

GREEN PEPPER

Rye Bread

BUTTER

S P

procedure:

1. knead together

2. chop and add

3. add and knead well

4. make into four fat disks

5. melt until brown

6. fry each side according to desired rareness

7. serve

50

potatoes here's spuds in your eye

baked

ingredients:

procedure:

1. scrub and dry

2. rub all over

3. bake

4. split

5. add

6. sprinkle and serve

potatoes à l'onion

ingredients:

Canned White POTATOES   onion   *BUTTER*   *PAPRIKA*   S

procedure:

1. melt

2. chop and add   3. open and drain

4. add

5. sprinkle—cook till light tan—serve

fried à la France

ingredients:

procedure:

1. peel

2. slice

3. soak in cold water

4. dry well

towel

5. heat till smoking

6. add—cook till tan

7. remove— drain on paper

8. sprinkle and serve

53

salads containing the new, amazing medical discovery: chlorophyll

salade Walt Whitman

ingredients:

lettuce

water cress

endive

celery

French Dressing (see page 59)

Salad Oil

radishes

½ cucumber

garlic

tangy hard cheese

procedure:

Salad Oil

1. pour

2. rub all over

3. cut up

4. add— use entire head

5. cut into small pieces

6. add and toss—serve

54

salade Roquefort serves four

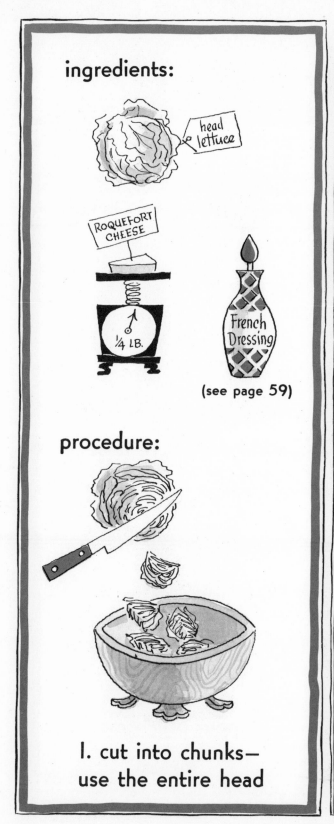

ingredients:

head lettuce

ROQUEFORT CHEESE

¼ LB.

French Dressing

(see page 59)

procedure:

1. cut into chunks—
use the entire head

2. break up and add

French Dressing

3. add—toss well—serve

asparagus salad

ingredients:

procedure:

1. beat till thick

2. add and mix in

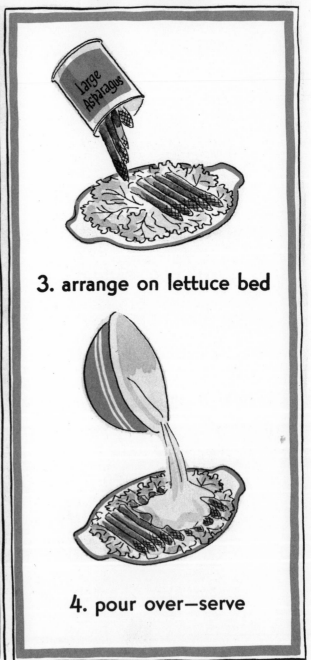

3. arrange on lettuce bed

4. pour over—serve

salade subversive

ingredients:   (see page 60)

procedure:

1. cut two wedges

2. cut into quarters

3. arrange thusly

4. pour over—serve

les choux froids cole slaw to you

ingredients:

procedure:

1. mix

2. add and mix

3. and

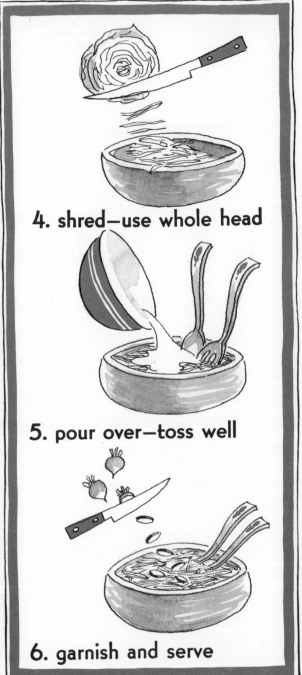

4. shred—use whole head

5. pour over—toss well

6. garnish and serve

French dressing—ou, la, la

ingredients:

Salad Oil · Vinegar · Dry Mustard · PAPRIKA · Empty Jar · S · P

procedure:

1. put   2. add   3. and

4. add few shakes   5. let stand   6. shake well

Russian  dressing—ach Karl, what you missed!

ingredients:

Mayonnaise Chili Sauce CATSUP Horse-Radish CAVIAR CHIVES P

procedure:

1. mix

2. and

3. and

4. mix well—serve

Russian Dressing

midsupper's night dream

LONG toward midnight, when conversation is limping and tongues idly flopping, and the heat's off, and the fire's burned out, and your guests are drooping over their chairs like Dali's limp clocks—there's a way to resurrect rather than bury them.

Creep off to your kitchenette; whip up one of these suggested dishes. Lusterless eyes will sparkle again, tongues clack with vivacity, and sufficient energy will have been imbued in your guests to enable them to eventually put on their coats and depart with a pleasant after-image in their minds—and tummies.

Welsh rabbit   serves four

ingredients:

American Cheese

1 LB.

WOR-CESTER-SHIRE SAUCE

BEER

Dry Mustard

RED Pepper

PAPRIKA

TOAST

procedure:

1. trim

2. keep warm

200°

3. start melting slowly—
do not allow to boil

4. add

5. cheese almost melted—add

6. stir until absorbed

7. remove—pour over—
sprinkle—serve

salmon salad Marguerite

for a hot night

ingredients:

procedure:

1. mix

2. chop and add

3. add

4. and mix in

5. garnish and serve

hot snack Marie serves four

ingredients:

procedure:

1. defrost—separate pieces

2. toast—one side only

3. place—toasted side down

4. slice into four pieces—place

5. add

6. broil till cheese is melted

follies minuit

serves 4

ingredients:

procedure:

1. boil
10 min.

2. meanwhile melt

3. add and stir

4. add and stir until thick

5. add

6. mix separately

66

7. dip both sides

8. fry till crisp

9. fry in bacon fat
until crusty

10. toast

11. combine

12. pour over—serve

casserole chien chaud
franks and beans to you

ingredients:

Serves 4
Takes 1 hr.

Baked Beans

HOT DOGS

Dry Mustard

CATSUP

Brown SUGAR

Casserole dish

procedure:

1. put in one-third of can only

2. slice in three and put in

3. cover with second one-third

4. add

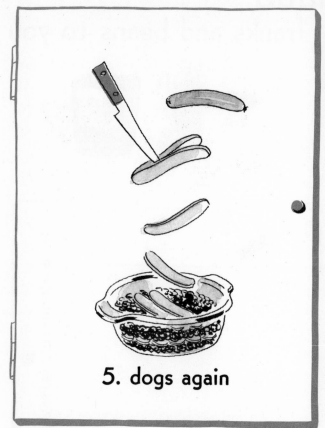

5. dogs again

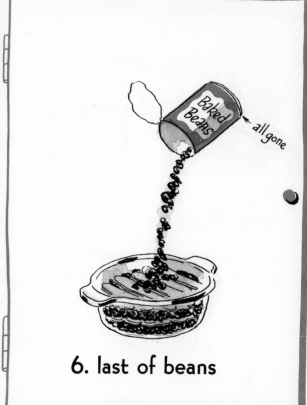

6. last of beans

7. sprinkle and cover with

8. bake and serve

spareribs barbecue

ingredients:

procedure:

1. cut into two rib sections—broil until brown—remove

2. heat

3. slice fine—fry till tan

4. add

70

5. and

6. and—simmer

7. pour over one-half

8. bake
baste with balance of
sauce while baking

crêpes suzettes

or—chafing just a bit (if you lack a chafing dish, substitute a deep frying pan)   serves four

ingredients:

FLOUR XXX · SUGAR · Cream · BUTTER · OLIVE OIL · Vanilla · Lemon · Orange · Powdered Sugar · S · COINTREAU · COGNAC

procedure:

1. beat together

2. add, sifted, and beat

3. add, grated

4. add, melted, and beat in

5. meanwhile heat

6. each crêpe 3″ in diameter

7. repeat hot oil, etc. for each batch—a total of twelve

8. crêpes done— put aside—melt in chafing dish

9. add, grated

10. and

over

11. and

12. put in—
cook till
sauce is
very syrupy

13. then
roll and
sprinkle

14. add

15. ignite

16. gloat
and serve
three per

fresh-air fodder

or picnics and barbecues

COME spring, come summer, come sunshine in the air and man sometimes likes to forego the comforts of cave dwelling to risk the rigors of ants, dust, dirt, and sand. Armed with picnic basket, charcoal, grill, suitable fodder, and, in company of mate or friend, he makes for the open spaces. He gathers wood, lights a fire, spreads a blanket, and tries to recreate, under the most trying of conditions, all the delights and pleasures of indoor eating — equipped with double the appetite and a fraction of the facilities.

The motto for this type of gastronomic gyration might well be "It's smart to be sticky." No matter "how you slice it," no one ever emerges from a fresh-air gustatory foray unscathed, unscarred, or unspotted.

The hazards of the open hearth are many, even for the hardy. Whether on the beach, in the back yard, on the plain, or in the woods, to maintain your status of he-man of the hearth, to avoid gremlins in your grill, there's a minimum of savoir-faire for picnic fare. So — to be an outdoor expert of the alimentary canal, peek on.

75

cold spread
for the torrid 90°

delicatessen special

ingredients:

RUSSIAN RYE · SWISS · SAUER-KRAUT · MUSTARD · RUSSIAN DRESSING (see page 60) · corned beef

procedure:

1. slice

2. place

3. spread lightly

4. put on — corned beef slice

5. pour over

6. cover—slice—wrap — wax ←paper

76

stuffed eggs

ingredients:

procedure:

1. boil and cool

2. shell—slice in half

3. remove yolks

4. add

5. and add

6. blend thoroughly

7. replace into whites—garnish

8. join and wrap

pickle-beef sandwich

ingredients:

slice roast beef

dill

MUSTARD

leaf lettuce

RYE

procedure:

1. slice

2. spread lightly

3. place

4. pickle sliced thin

5. place and garnish

6. cover—cut in half—wrap

78

cheese fingers

ingredients:

procedure:

1. mix

2. chop—add—mix in

3. trim; cut into inch strips

4. spread thickly—cover—wrap

salad sandwich

ingredients:    (see page 60)

procedure:

1. spread

2. put on

3. slice and place on

4. add

5. and

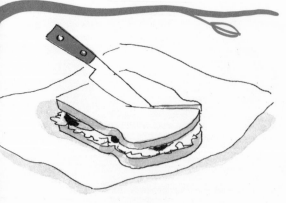

6. cover—slice—wrap

picnic punch

ingredients:

oranges — or MEDOC — WHITE BORDEAUX — SODA — MARASCHINO CHERRIES — SUGAR

procedure:

1. empty   THERMOS

2. add   THERMOS

3. and   THERMOS

4. and
(juice only)   THERMOS

5. add—stir well   THERMOS

6. garnish—cap   THERMOS

81

cooking

with ozone

steak grillée

ingredients:

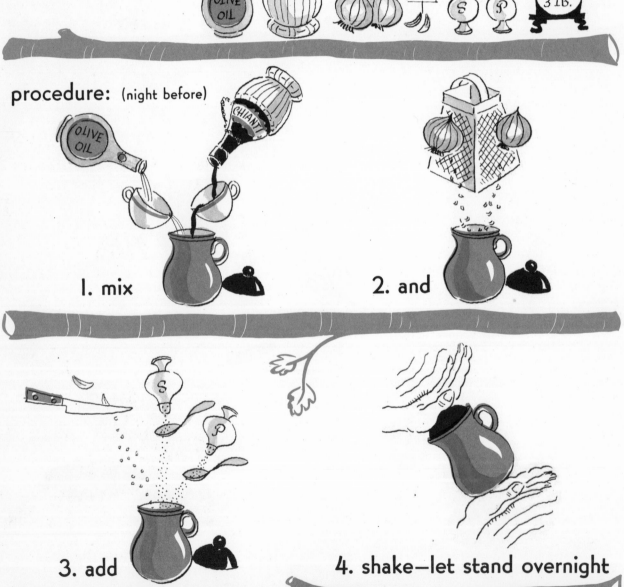

procedure: (night before)

1. mix

2. and

3. add

4. shake—let stand overnight

procedure: (next day)

5. build wood fire—add

6. when coals glow, sear
each side rapidly

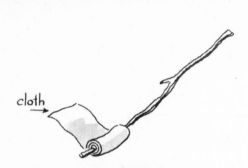

cloth

7. make baster so

8. dip

9. baste each side

10. cook ten to twenty
minutes—serve

corn on the coals

ingredients:

procedure:

1. soak   ½ hr.

2. meanwhile—build fire and allow hot ashes to accumulate

3. bury corn in ashes

4. remove after ½ hr. strip husks

5. serve so

bread Français

ingredients:

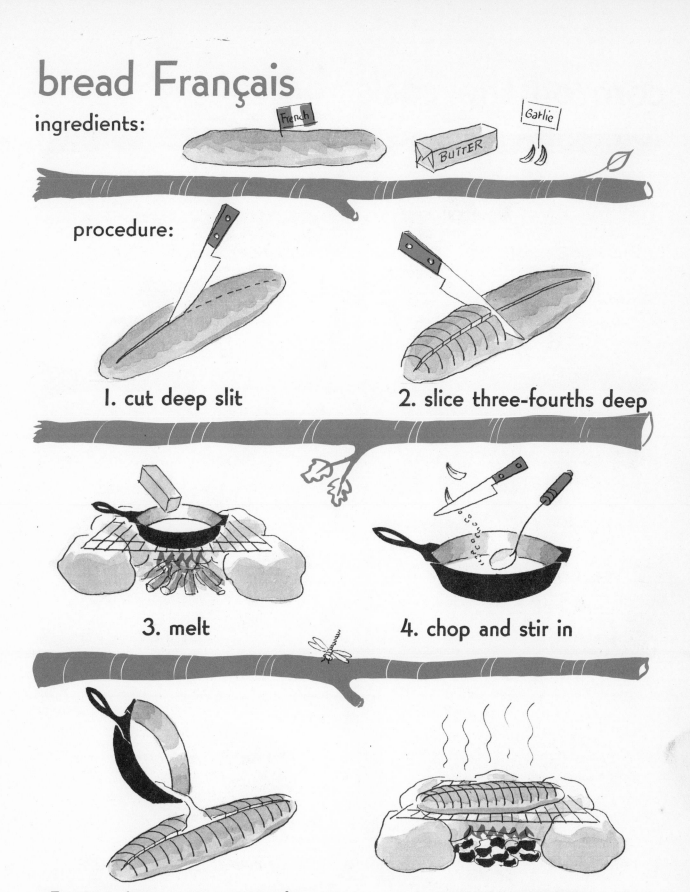

procedure:

1. cut deep slit

2. slice three-fourths deep

3. melt

4. chop and stir in

5. pour into center trench

6. toast—serve hot

the hot banana

ingredients:

procedure:

1. (do not peel)—make three-inch slit in skin

2. put in slit

3. place—turn each side cook (8 min.) serve

barbecued tomatoes

ingredients:

procedure: (night before)

1. mix—let soak overnight

2. cut in half—baste

3. grill and baste—serve

the solid teaser

—the cocktail canape

THIS interesting gastronomic teaser is a paradox in every way. It does not whet one's appetite — but, instead, serves to whet one's thirst. The more you eat, the more you drink, which, combined, decreases your gustatory needs. *Quel* paradox!

This predicament has several advantages for the host: when serving cocktails before dinner, it will tend to cut down on unexpected inroads on your main repast. And canapés at cocktailtime tend to keep your guests on an even keel (albeit at the expense of your liquor supply).

Anyway, there is the canapé and as a host you've got to do better than just serving toast, or peanuts, or popcorn to lend éclat to your efforts.

So here's to the canapé — the cocktail snack — the midget meal — the salivary titillator — the drink-whetter and appetite-forgetter.

c'est la vie canapé

ingredients:

procedure:

1. mash

2. add and make paste

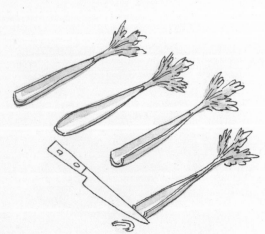

3. cut and separate stalks

4. fill each stalk

canapé fromage and strictly from hunger

ingredients:

procedure:

fruit glass

1. cut out like so and toast

2. mix into paste

3. add and mix in

4. add finely chopped

5. spread—sprinkle for color

6. serve

urgéd **sturgeon canapé**

ingredients:

procedure:

1. hard boil and cool

2. then chop very fine

3. mix separately

4. add and mix

5. cut out and toast

6. spread and sprinkle over each

7. serve

shrimp à la Marx canapé

ingredients:

5 oz. SHRIMPS · Russian Dressing (see page 60) · TOOTHPICKS

procedure:

1. drain

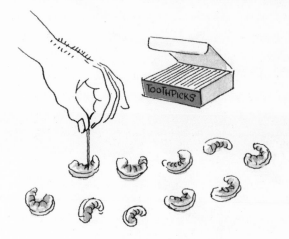

2. impale each

3. pour into glass bowl

4. arrange so

canapé olive chaud

ingredients:

procedure:

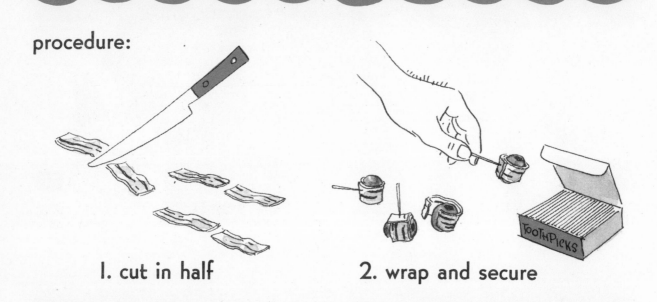

1. cut in half

2. wrap and secure

3. broil

4. remove and serve pronto

PART VII

drinks

the host's liquid assets

YOU can lead a guest to water but you can't make him drink — not if it's firewater he wants. And — a guest can lead his host to the bar but can't make him mix a drink either — not if he doesn't know how.

How do we know? Surveys, of course! There's been the Gallup Poll and the Roper Poll and the Kinsey Report, and now there's the BINGEY REPORT, conducted solely to compile the data for our subject matter, liquid hosting. In the process of this survey we uncovered some of the most amazing facts about the drinking habits germane to the American male:

1. He will experiment with utter abandon with a variety of drink methods — when at a bar.

2. He will even encourage his companion to experiment with the drink fantastic, and is as adventuresome as any red-blooded pioneer of old —when at a bar.

3. When this identical bold adventurer is at home and is confronted with mixing anything other than a whiskey straight (or with soda), he's as a timid as a bride (of old).

4. 96.8% OF AMERICAN MALES ARE DRINK-TENDER VIRGINS.

The purpose, therefore, of this entire section is to introduce the adult male to the true facts of fermentation so it can be enjoyed with the maximum of tempered pleasure.

After a very profound (but delightful) study, verified by the terrifying conclusions of the BINGEY survey, here is the basic law of liquids which, in its way, is just as vital as Boyle's Law concerning gaseous matter:

LAW OF LIQUID REFRESHMENT (especially those fermented): *Omnis drinks divisaesunt in partes quinque!* Using a standard "pony," this is translated as, "All drinks are divided into five parts":

1. Cocktail-hour drinks
2. Before-dinner drinks
3. Drinks with meals
4. After-dinner drinks
5. Drinks that have nothing to do with meals (for card parties, social gatherings, and general conviviality)

For further details, read on —

this is what you need in way of basic fuel

basic implements

cocktail shaker

Squeezer

spoon and opener

corkscrew

jigger

ice strainer

muddler

ice-cube bowl

basic containers

cocktail

Collins

Highball

Old Fashioned

Drink

Cognac

Liqueur

coasters

Sherry

Here are all the measuring symbols you have to know:

——————————— jigger (1¾ oz.)

½ ——————— half-jigger

——————— teaspoon

——————— half-teaspoon

|110| ——————— a dash of

Note all recipes are for one drink only - multiply where necessary

dissolving the five o'clock shadow

or the cocktail hour

PEOPLE are strange. When you invite them for cocktails, they expect cocktails — they are unreasonable that way. But what's even more strange, there's many a host who makes this grandiose invitation: "Drop over for a cocktail around five." And what happens? The guest arrives, parched and expectant, and is offered his choice of whiskey and water or soda. That the host's entire repertoire.

The moral of this story is: when you do invite guests for cocktails, remember — they expect cocktails. And — all you have to do to be able to shake — or stir — a potent potable is to read on and follow the pictures.

horse's neck really

ingredients:

1. peel and drape

2. add

3. add—fill—serve

whiskey sour

ingredients:

1. squeeze—add

2. add and shake

3. pour— garnish—serve

orange blossom

ingredients:

1. mix

2. add and shake

3. pour—garnish

daiquiri

ingredients:

1. mix

2. add shake till frosted

3. pour—serve

sidecar

ingredients:

1. separate and beat white only

2. mix

3. add shaved ice— shake till frosty

piscolabis

ingredients:

1. crack and fill

2. add

3. stir—garnish— serve

bluebell

ingredients:

1. mix
2. add
3. shake—serve

comin' thro' the rye

ingredients:

1. mix
2. add
3. pour—serve

rob roy

ingredients:

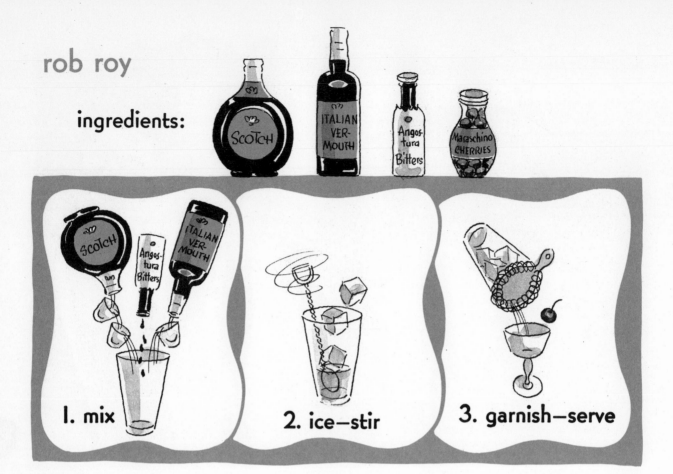

1. mix

2. ice—stir

3. garnish—serve

rum and maple
ingredients:

1. mix

2. add

3. shake—serve

before-dinner drinks

aperitifs and cocktails

WHY drinks before meals?

Whether you're host to one or one hundred, no matter the sex involved, each must be wooed like a woman, gently, subtly, and with perfect timing and priming. For a guest, newly arrived at your home, is a xenophobic animal, on edge with suspicions and fears: his host may have Borgia tendencies at mealtime. The other guests may be an insidious mixture of pickpockets, undercover agents, rakes, and/or adventuresses — or worse still — all bores.

But ply this quivering creature with just the right kind of drink and he becomes calm, conversational, convivial, and most receptive to both your guests and to your efforts as a host. So here are the requisites for wooing your dinner guest, as you prime his salivaries.

103

bacardi cocktail

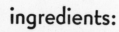

ingredients:

1. mix 2. shake 3. serve

bamboo cocktail

ingredients:

1. mix 2. shake 3. serve

brandy cocktail

ingredients:

1. add to shaker half full of shaved ice

2. add and stir well

3. pour and twist

Bronx cocktail

ingredients:

1. mix

2. shake

3. pour and add

Delmonico cocktail

ingredients:

1. mix   2. ice—stir   3. pour

Manhattan cocktail

ingredients:

1. mix   2. ice—stir   3. pour and add

Martini cocktail

ingredients:

1. mix

2. ice—stir very thoroughly

3. pour—add

subversive Martini cocktail

ingredients:

1. mix

2. ice—stir

3. pour and twist

Martini esoterica
cocktail

ingredients:

1. mix

2. ice—stir *well*

3. pour and add

old fashioned
cocktail

ingredients:

1. muddle

2. add and muddle

**3. add—
stir—garnish**

PART X

drinks with meals

or how to float a dessert

 jug of wine, a loaf of bread — and thou beside me singing in the wilderness."

A delightful situation.

But if thou, bud, doth not have the correct wine with the loaf, thou wilt be singing in the wilderness — alone!

Did you know, for example, that white wine with steak is a faux pas; that red wine with chicken may be a subversive gaucherie; that beer with dessert is a capital crime?

The correct drinks to serve with meals is a very ticklish subject. Your entire social future can be destroyed by not knowing what to serve with what. So to spare you such an anchorite, antisocial dilemma, here is a chart to guide you through the unchartered Sahara of an eight-course meal—right through dessert.

109

wine	with	wine temperature

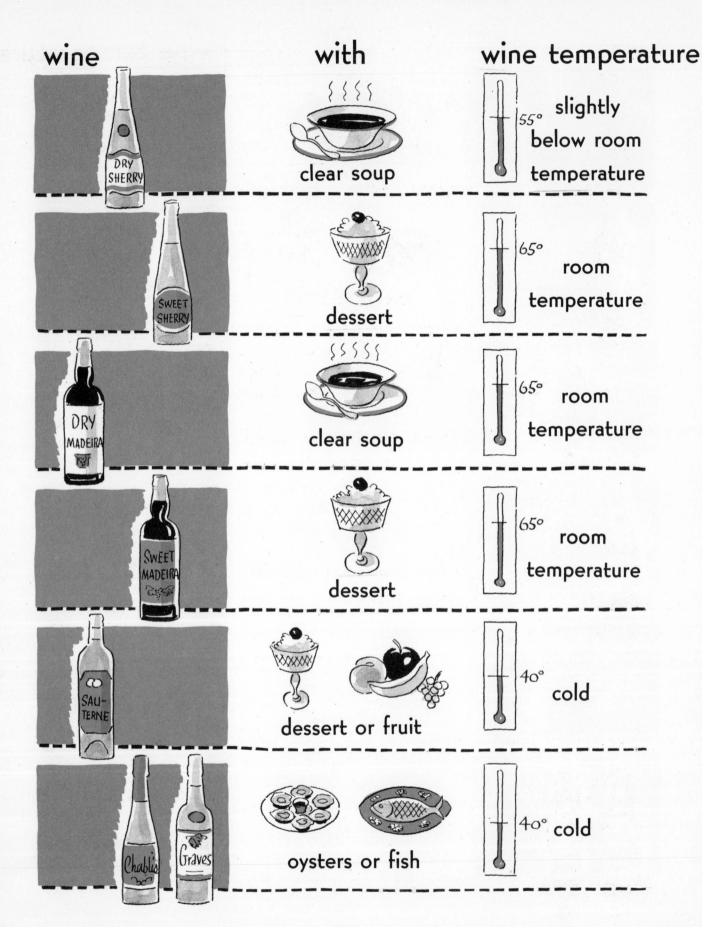

DRY SHERRY — clear soup — 55° slightly below room temperature

SWEET SHERRY — dessert — 65° room temperature

DRY MADEIRA — clear soup — 65° room temperature

SWEET MADEIRA — dessert — 65° room temperature

SAUTERNE — dessert or fruit — 40° cold

Chablis **Graves** — oysters or fish — 40° cold

wine	with	wine temperature
RHINE Moselle	fish	45° below room temperature
RED Burgundy	steak or venison	65° room temperature
CLARET CHIANTI	roast, chicken, or salad	65° room temperature
DRY Champagne	fish (also entire meal)	32°
PORT	cheese	65° room temperature
Malaga Muscatel	dessert	65° room temperature

after-dinner drinks

A well-fed after-dinner guest is a fatted calf — ready for the slow torture of postprandial discomfort. His eyes are glazed, his mind is dazed — he's an inert maze of gastrointestinal activity.

But there's a cure. It's continental, elemental, and an extremely cordial form of resuscitation — with liqueur.

There are more cordials on the market than there are nationalities. On the following pages, however, are depicted only those which have the international stamp of approval. And no esoteric legerdemain is required to serve them other than an ample supply — and some liqueur glasses. Only in a few instances is any form of mixing a requisite.

So to resurrect your sluggish guest — pour on.

your liqueur store

the liqueur glass
for all cordials shown
except cognac

the brandy glass
for cognac
snifting

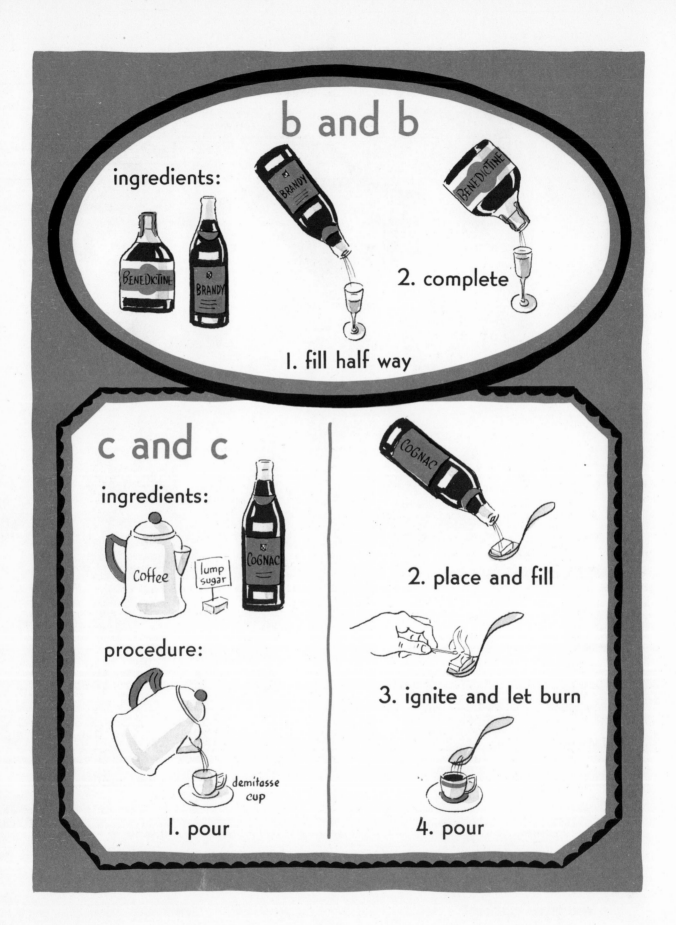

b and b

ingredients:

1. fill half way

2. complete

c and c

ingredients:

Coffee

lump sugar

COGNAC

procedure:

1. pour

demitasse cup

2. place and fill

3. ignite and let burn

4. pour

114

drinks that have nothing to do with meals

THIS is the last chapter, the last verse, on drink etiquette.

Liquors were not merely brewed and fermented to abet one's gustatory powers. A drink, partaken of with proper discretion, acts as a pleasant thirst-quencher, a chill-destroyer, and a social-cementer. Served at card parties, dances, or even gatherings of intellectual pundits, it releases tensions and dissolves unnecessary taboos.

In fact, an alcoholic beverage is a social cyclotron breaking down the self-contained atoms (your guests) and dispersing the neutrons, deuterons, electrons, and persons equitably so that a pleasant mixture of personalities results.

So when a crowd descends upon you for an evening of bridge or poker, or just for conviviality at your expense, do you know what to serve? Or on a long, hot summer's afteroon, what to quaff? Or on a bleak, black winter's day, what to snift?

Read on.

beer
(hot or cold weather)

pour tilted

Bourbon highball (cold weather)

ingredients:

1. pour

2. add

brandy highball (cold weather)

ingredients:

1. pour

2. add

champagne punch (hot or cold weather—you won't know the difference)

ingredients:

oranges · Champagne · Champagne · APRICOT BRANDY · VODKA · lemons · peaches

serves 8 or more

procedure:

1. squeeze

2. add

3. pour and stir

4. slice—garnish—serve

block of ice

ICE CUBES

eggnog

for eggmas cheer (cold weather)

ingredients:

serves 8 or more

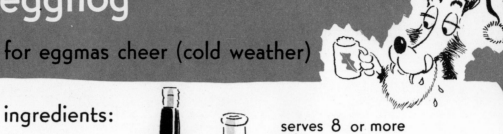

procedure:

1. separate and beat each

2. add and beat in

3. and beat in

4. stir in gently and sprinkle

Cuban cola (hot weather)

ingredients:

procedure:

1. squeeze—add

2. add—stir—serve

French "75"
(hot weather)

ingredients:

procedure:

1. squeeze

2. add

3. fill—stir—quaff

mint julep (hot weather)

ingredients:

mint   Bourbon   SUGAR   shaved ice

procedure:

1. crush

2. add and crush

3. add and crush

4. pack solid—add

5. juggle—stir
until frost forms on
outside of glass

6. garnish—sip

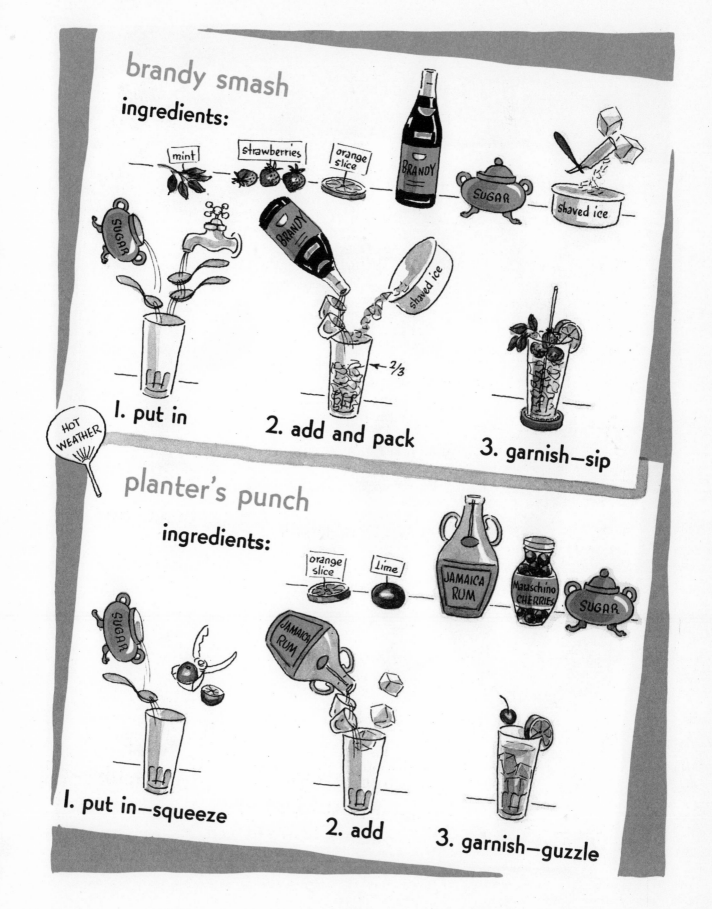

brandy smash

ingredients:

mint | strawberries | orange slice | BRANDY | SUGAR | shaved ice

HOT WEATHER

1. put in

2. add and pack

←2/3

3. garnish—sip

planter's punch

ingredients:

orange slice | lime | JAMAICA RUM | Maraschino CHERRIES | SUGAR

1. put in—squeeze

2. add

3. garnish—guzzle

rum Collins

ingredients:

1. put in and squeeze

2. add

3. add—serve

HOT WEATHER

Tom Collins

ingredients:

1. put in and squeeze

2. add

3. add—serve

Scotch and soda
(hot or cold weather)

ingredients:

1. put in

2. add and serve

rye highball
(hot or cold weather)

ingredients:

1. put in

2. add and serve

index

index